I0821051

Anglerfish and Other STRANGE Deep-Sea Creatures

by Rachel Rose

Bearport Books, an imprint of Bearport Publishing by FlutterBee

Credits

Cover and title page, © Diego Grandi/Shutterstock and © Kelvin Aitken/VWPics/Alamy Stock Photo and © Solvin Zankl/Alamy Stock Photo; 3, © OpenCage/Wikimedia and © Dianne Bray/Museum Victoria/Wikimedia and © lapis2380/Adobe Stock; 4–5, © Deep Slope 2007/NOAA–OE and © Neil Bromhall/Shutterstock and © diegograndi/Adobe Stock and © Scenessence/Adobe Stock and © Kuznetsov Petr/Shutterstock; 6, © Marko Steffensen/Alamy Stock Photo; 6–7, © Nature Picture Library/Alamy Stock Photo; 7BR, © Nature Picture Library/Alamy Stock Photo; 8, © Solvin Zankl/Alamy Stock Photo; 8–9, © Steve Downer/Science Source; 9BL, © Steve Downer/Science Source; 10, © Premaphotos/Alamy Stock Photo; 10–11, © Norbert Wu/Minden Pictures; 12, © hyotographics/Shutterstock; 12–13, © Brandon Cole Marine Photography/Alamy Stock Photo; 13BL, © Joel Sartore/Photo Ark/NPL/Minden Pictures; 14, © David Shen/Blue Planet Archive; 14–15, © Marko Steffensen/Alamy Stock Photo; 16, © Alessandro Mancini/Alamy Stock Photo; 16–17, © Deep Slope 2006/NOAA–OE; 18, © mauritius images GmbH/Alamy Stock Photo; 18–19, © Nature Picture Library/Alamy Stock Photo; 19BL, © Mark Conlin/VWPics/Alamy Stock Photo; 20, © Kyodo/AP Images; 20–21, © Yiming Chen/Getty Images; 22, © IanDagnall Computing/Alamy Stock Photo; 23, © Wikimedia

Bearport Publishing Company Product Development Team

Kayla Eggert, Theresa Emminizer, Kim Jones, Allison Juda, Cole Nelson, Naomi Reich, Steve Scheluchin, Tiana Tran

Statement on Usage of Generative Artificial Intelligence

Bearport Publishing remains committed to publishing high-quality nonfiction books. Therefore, we restrict the use of generative AI to ensure accuracy of all text and visual components pertaining to a book's subject. See BearportPublishing.com for details.

Library of Congress Cataloging-in-Publication Data is available at www.loc.gov or upon request from the publisher.

ISBN: 979-8-89577-628-5 (hardcover)
ISBN: 979-8-89577-716-9 (ebook)

For more information, write to Bearport Publishing, 3500 American Blvd W, Suite 150, Bloomington, MN 55431. Printed in the United States of America.

CONTENTS

A Glowing Trap

In the deepest, darkest parts of the ocean, there's a world of wild and wacky animals. At 650 feet (200 m) underwater there's no light from the sun—only what comes from creatures themselves.

The anglerfish glows eerily in the dark. Its light dangles just in front of huge, round eyes and sharp, scary teeth. Let's dive into the cold, creepy world of anglerfish and other deep-sea creatures.

Anglerfish

The anglerfish is looking for a bite. It reaches a fishing rod-like body part from its head and lights up the squishy tip, hoping to attract **prey**. Wiggling this bait, the anglerfish waits patiently for a meal to swim up. When prey is within reach, it opens its jaw wide and . . . *Snap!* Dinner is served.

There are more than 200 kinds of deep-sea anglerfish. One is called the black seadevil.

A black seadevil

Anglerfish live in what's called the midnight zone, 3,000–13,000 feet (900–4,000 m) deep in the ocean.
Female anglerfish are often much larger than males.
Sometimes, a **male** anglerfish will attach itself to a female and live off her for food!
A male anglerfish

Vampire Squid

Despite its name, this scary underwater oddity doesn't want to suck your blood. It isn't a vampire! But with its cape-like arms and big, red eyes, it sure looks like one. The cape even has pointy parts that look like vampire fangs.

There's very little **oxygen** where vampire squid live. Their large gills help them take in the oxygen they need from the water.

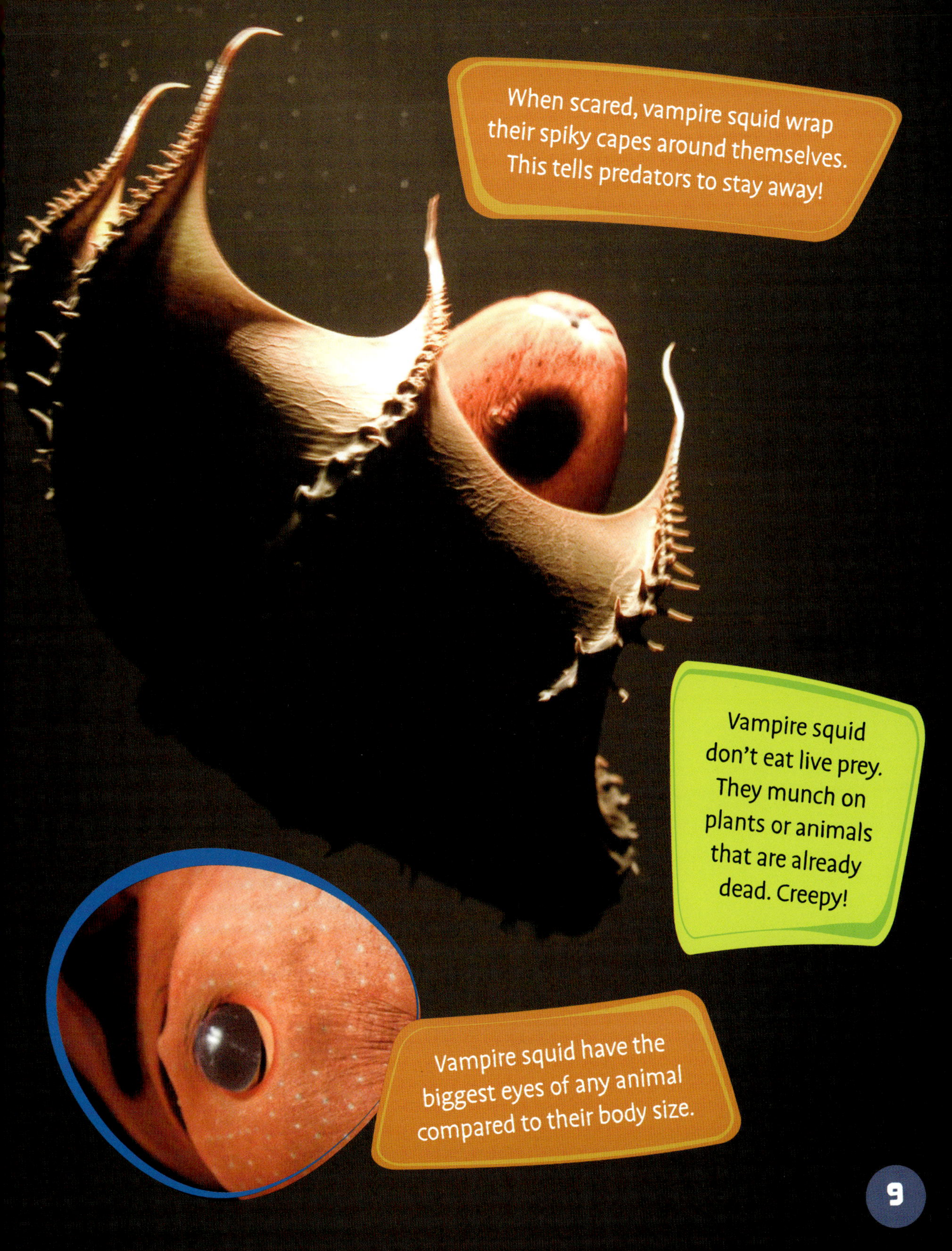

When scared, vampire squid wrap their spiky capes around themselves. This tells predators to stay away!

Vampire squid don't eat live prey. They munch on plants or animals that are already dead. Creepy!

Vampire squid have the biggest eyes of any animal compared to their body size.

Giant Sea Spider

The giant sea spider is no itsy-bitsy spider. In fact, with its long spindly legs, this huge creepy crawler can grow up to 28 inches (71 cm) wide. That's bigger than a dinner plate! But don't worry. Since this critter lives at depths of up to 13,100 ft. (4,000 m), it's unlikely you'll ever see one. *Phew!*

Male giant sea spiders take care of their eggs until they **hatch**.

Eggs

Although they're called spiders, these ocean dwellers are a different kind of animal than the spiders you see on land.

Some of a giant sea spider's **organs** are found in its legs.

These legs are made for walking . . . and breathing! A giant sea spider breathes through **pores** in its legs.

Hagfish

Yuck! With their creepy eel-like bodies and gross slime, hagfish might make you gag! In fact, that's just how hagfish stay safe from predators. These jawless fish release slime to choke any animals that try to take a bite. Just one hagfish can make a whopping 6.3 gallons (20 L) of slime!

In Japan and Korea, people eat hagfish. It's thought of as a very special meal.

Hagfish are the only animals in the world that have a skull but no backbone.

Hagfish are blind. They depend on their strong senses of smell and touch to find food.

Goblin Shark

Look out! With their enormous see-through bodies and superlong noses, goblin sharks are spooky creatures in the deep, dark ocean. They can grow up to 12 ft. (3.6 m) long and weigh up to 460 pounds (210 kg). Underneath their big honkers, these underwater goblins have huge jaws with rows and rows of sharp teeth—all the better to eat their prey with!

When hunting, a goblin shark can shoot its toothy jaw out like a slingshot!

These sea creatures are sometimes called elfin sharks.
Goblin sharks look pink because of the blood flowing beneath their see-through skin.
Goblin sharks have been swimming in the deep sea for more than 125 million years.

Giant Isopod

Yikes! What is that huge, shelled, many-legged creature that looks like an underwater bug? It's a giant isopod! About the size of a bowling pin, one of the reasons these **crustaceans** may have grown so big is because they don't have many predators where they live at the bottom of the ocean. Any animal that does try to take a bite will be disappointed. Giant isopods don't have much meat to them.

Giant isopods feel around in the dark with long **antennae**.

An antenna

Giant isopods have 14 legs.
They grow up to 16 in. (41 cm) long!
There are more than 10,000 kinds of isopods living in water and on land. The giant isopod is the largest.

Dragonfish

With its glowing body, big head, and fang-like teeth, the unearthly dragonfish can be found lurking in the deepest, darkest parts of the ocean. Many kinds of dragonfish are almost black in color and make their own light, giving off an eerie red or blue glow. This brings curious prey close enough to catch. *Eek!*

The dragonfish's fangs are see-through. This makes it hard for prey to spot the sharp teeth!

Dragonfish live in the midnight zone, and some can go as far down as 14,800 ft. (4,500 m), into the abyssal zone.

At night, dragonfish swim to the **surface** of the water to feed on the small fish and plankton there.

Deep-sea dragonfish are typically small, growing to around 6 in. (15 cm). Females are often larger than males.

Deep-Sea Discoveries

From vampires and dragons to goblins and giants, the deepest, darkest parts of the ocean are filled with strange beings. Scientists haven't fully explored the deepest zones of the ocean yet, so there may be even more to discover! When new tools help us reach these places, what wild and wonderful creatures will we find?

Like most deep-sea creatures, blobfish have soft and squishy bodies. This helps them withstand the **pressure** deep in the ocean.

The Japanese porcupine crab is covered in sharp spikes! *Ouch!*
Many deep-sea animals move slowly. This helps them save energy.

MEET AN UNDERWATER RESEARCHER

Sylvia Earl is one of the most well known **marine biologists**. She holds the record for the deepest walk on the sea floor ever! With all that she has seen, Sylvia works hard to protect the oceans. She started a group called Mission Blue that works to make the oceans clean and safe for the animals living there.

As a child, Sylvia spent hours playing in her backyard pond, which was filled with fish and tadpoles.

GLOSSARY

antennae feelers on top of the heads of some animals; the singular of antennae is antenna

crustaceans a group of animals, including giant isopods, crabs, and lobsters, that have a hard shell and no backbone

female an animal that can lay eggs or give birth to babies

hatch to come out of an egg

male an animal that can't lay eggs or give birth to babies

marine biologists scientists who study the oceans and the creatures that live in them

organs body parts that do a particular job

oxygen a colorless gas found in air and water that animals breathe

pores tiny holes in an animal's skin

pressure a pressing force put on something

prey animals that are hunted by other animals for food

surface the top or outer layer of something

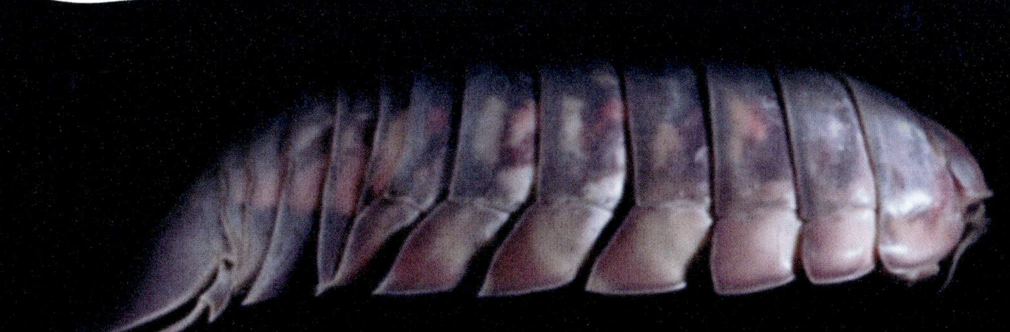

INDEX

READ MORE

Hall, Alex. *Ocean Habitats (Habitats)*. Mendota, MN: North Star Editions, 2025.

Rose, Rachel. *Goblin Shark (Shark Shock!)*. Minneapolis: Bearport Publishing, 2022.

LEARN MORE ONLINE

1. Go to **FactSurfer.com** or scan the QR code below.
2. Enter "**Deep-Sea Creatures**" into the search box.
3. Click on the cover of this book to see a list of websites.

About the Author

Rachel Rose lives in San Francisco. Her favorite thing to do there is to dip in the bay, where she swims with a lot of playful seals.